A Message From Sam

Nancy K. Schriefer

Escape
Key
Press™

St. Paul, Minnesota

Escape
Key
Press™

A Division of Prism Marketing, Inc.

245 East 6th Street
St. Paul, Minnesota 55101

This book is a work of fiction. Names, characters, places and incidents are products of the author's imagination. Any resemblance to actual events or locales or persons, living or dead, is entirely coincidental.

Copyright © 1996 by Nancy K. Schriefer
All rights reserved, including the right of reproduction in whole or in part in any form.

Grateful acknowledgement is made to the following for permission to reprint previously published material.
I'll Be There, by John Cristoforou, John Holliday, Trevor Steel, Milan Zekavica © 1991 Love Pump Music Ltd., All Rights administered by Warner-Tamerlane Publishing Corp.
All Rights Reserved, Used by Permission
WARNER BROS. PUBLICATIONS U.S. INC. Miami, FL 33014

On Eagle's Wings, by Michael Joncas
© 1979, 1991 New Dawn Music
5536 N. E. Hassalo, Portland, OR 97213
All Rights Reserved, Used by Permission

Escape Key Press is a trademark
of Prism Marketing, Inc.

Designed by Patricia Gardner Design
St. Paul, Minnesota

Manufactured in the United States of America

ISBN 0-9651274-7-8

*For my daughter, Kris,
whom I love and miss…lots and lots.*

Don't be afraid, my love,
I'll be watching you from above...
I may have died, but I've gone nowhere,
Just think of me and I'll be there.

— John Christoforou et. al.

Pat McGrew's mind rambled. She'd been focusing on a candle flame during the eulogy, trying to stay in control. But when she heard Bob's voice crack, as he said, "Steven Albert McGrew, our dear friend Sam, will live forever in our hearts," she jerked abruptly back to the moment and a tremor ripped through her body. She felt Mac's vain attempt at comfort, her son's arm draping her shaking shoulders as he enveloped her in grief of his own. It's impossible, she thought. It just can't be.

Bob Anders, the McGrews' neighbor, lawyer and half of their favorite couple, stepped down from the podium, casting a solemn glance Pat's way, and joined his wife in the first pew across the aisle. Father Cooper took his place and began his homily. "We've gathered here today to celebrate the beginning of Sam's new life in God's kingdom."

I can't listen to this, Pat thought. She turned her tear-laden eyes toward the skylights over the altar and stared at the deep blue autumn sky beyond. "Dear God, help me," she prayed, her lips forming the words silently. Then, "dear Sam, why did you leave me?"

Another sob wracked her being and her eyes over-flowed. She sniffed and searched the pockets of her black crepe suit but found only wet tissues. Sensing her mother's need through her own tears, Anne peeled two dry ones from the bundle she was carrying and handed them to Pat. Then she turned to answer her own daughter, Allison, who sang out sadly from her father's arms in the pew behind, "why is Nana crying?"

"We can't talk in church, baby," Anne whispered to her three-year-old as Pat turned her tear-stained face toward the child and reached for her hand.

"I love you, Nana," Ali continued in a loud whisper. "Where's my Papa?"

"Where, indeed?" Pat muttered, wiping her eyes.

"We shouldn't have brought her to the church," Anne apologized.

"It's okay," her mother whispered, squeezing her daughter's hand as the priest continued.

A MESSAGE FROM SAM

Pat glanced toward the white draped casket that stood in the center of the church. How can this be, she thought again. What day is this, Thursday? Just four days ago we sat here together listening to Father Cooper's sermon. He talked about the harvest and about gathering graces. And now I'm here alone and you're there . . . where? The tears started again.

It had happened Monday. Pat had her usual session with Maria at the literacy project. Later she had volunteered at the library's used book sale. She had never had an actual career outside her home. Being a wife and mother, though unusual these days, was exactly the life she wanted. But she used her English degree volunteering for anything that had to do with books. She loved reading and tried to share that love with everyone. And she had never needed to work.

Money was not an issue for Sam and Pat McGrew. They had met in college and married in the spring, just before graduation. Sam had found a good job as an accountant at a manufacturing company, spent his entire career there and had worked his way up to chief financial officer. They'd had the average American family, a daughter and a son, put them both through college, and had been looking forward to early retirement in a few years.

Oh, the plans they had made. Long car trips through the national parks, visiting their children, one on each coast, spending summers at the cabin and winters on the gulf or in the desert. It would be wonderful. They were happiest when they were together. And when Sam retired, they'd be together all the time. Just thinking about that had been a joy. But all those plans died Monday when Sam did . . . when that horrible call came.

Father was finishing his message when Pat turned her attention away from her husband's casket. The assembled group rose to respond to the priest's prayers. For Sam's soul, for his widow, his children, his grandchild, the congregation prayed. The funeral continued and during communion the soloist sang *Amazing Grace*, Sam's favorite hymn. Pat steeled herself against the emotion of the music by digging her heels into the floor. She held a hand of each of her children and fought for strength.

When the final blessing was given, the pallbearers, their friends, stood and formed two rows of three behind the casket. As the procession began its final march out of the church, the organ intoned the music Pat had selected as the recessional. She knew it well and tried to sing along, but her voice cracked and the words stuck in her throat. "*And He will raise you up, on eagle's wings, bear you on the breath of dawn, make you to shine like the sun, and hold you in the palm of His hand."* She had chosen this song because it reminded her of the lake, the sunrises and sunsets she and Sam had enjoyed and the presence of God they felt so strongly there.

"Dad would have liked this," Mac whispered to his mother as they made their way toward the back of the church.

"He had a lot of friends," she whispered back. "Look at this crowd. Even the atrium is full."

As the pallbearers lifted the casket into the hearse Pat joined Anne, her husband, Gregg, little Allison and Mac and his fiancée, Lisa, in a waiting car for the journey to the cemetery.

"I knew dad was a popular guy, but this is overwhelming," Anne said, looking back at the long string of cars pulling out of the church parking lot.

"I don't expect everyone to come to the cemetery," Pat said. "I really dislike that part. I always leave right after the church service to avoid it."

Anne drew in a shaky breath and reached over and patted her mother's hand. "Just hang in there a little longer, Mom. It'll be over soon."

Shortly, the hearse made a turn through the cemetery's old stone gate and the cortege followed, passing between rows of flaming maple trees and ancient marble monuments. Pat could see a tent set up beyond, somewhat apart from the other graves.

"Annie and I picked out a spot way up on the hill," Mac explained. "It seemed so peaceful there, I hope it's all right." Mac stopped the car a short distance behind the hearse, got out, opened his mother's door and took her hand.

"This is a beautiful spot," Pat agreed in hushed tones. "I'm grateful that you two took care of finding the plot. I just couldn't. Your father can be at peace here." She walked slowly toward the tent, her heels slipping into the soft earth with each step.

Banging car doors and a shrieking jay disturbed the somber silence. The crowd began to gather near the flower-ringed casket positioned over a gaping copper vault. Father Cooper waited until the last of the mourners made the trudge from their cars, up the hill on foot, before beginning his prayers.

"Heavenly Father, we thank you for this glorious day, for this beautiful season and for giving us Sam. He was truly a gift. But, as with all earthly gifts, only temporary. So now, at your behest, we give him back to you." Sprinkling the casket with holy water, he continued. "Earth to earth. Ashes to ashes. Dust to dust."

Pat gripped her mouth, squeezed her eyes and stifled a sob. Oh, God, she thought, why? Why now? I don't want to give him back to you. I need him here, with me.

The shrillness of the ringing phone invaded her thoughts.

"Mrs. McGrew?"

"Yes."

"This is Ruth Simms at County Medical Center calling."

"Yes, Ms. Simms, what can I do for you?"

"Is Steven McGrew your husband?"

"Yes."

Pat couldn't recall the next words. She couldn't even recollect hearing words. She only remembered sensations: trembling in her legs, pounding in her chest, coldness and an incredible emptiness. She sank to the floor in despair.

". . . Surely goodness and mercy will follow me all the days of my life and I will dwell in the house of the Lord forever." Father Cooper was nearly finished now.

"May your soul, Sam, and the souls of all the faithful departed, through the mercy of God, rest in peace."

"Amen," responded the gathering.

"Yes, rest, my love," Pat said, stepping forward,

"until forever." And placing a single red rose on the casket, she kissed the rich mahogany. She stepped back, glanced at the crowd and murmured, "thank you all for coming." Then turning, she walked back to the waiting car and lost all semblance of control.

♦

T he next two days blurred past. Pat tried to enjoy her children's company. She knew the visit would be short and that they'd soon be leaving for their homes and jobs. She dreaded the moment she'd truly be alone when she'd have to face the rest of her life. She paid particular attention to little Allison, who could not understand Papa's absence. Heaven was not comprehensible to the three-year-old who adored her grandfather.

There were constant interruptions: condolence calls, neighbors dropping by with food and more food, thank you notes to write, memorials to set up and the inevitable dealings with the attorney.

"The police would like you to review the accident report," Bob said when he stopped by for coffee Saturday morning. "They're preparing charges and they have some questions about Sam's running routine."

The loud, pulsating tone roused Pat from her bewil-

derment. She stared at the receiver still lying in her lap. She pulled herself up against the door frame, hung up the phone and walked slowly to the kitchen window. Drawing back the curtain, she stared out into the back yard. Katie Anders was across the way raking leaves. Pat opened her patio door and shouted to her friend, "Kate, I need you. It's Sam."

Katie dropped her rake and ran through the leaves to the McGrew's deck. "What is it? What about Sam?" she asked, concern overtaking her as she got close enough to see Pat's face.

"County Med Center called. He was out running. There was some sort of accident."

"I'll drive you. Get your purse. I'll call Bob and have him meet us."

"Paa-aat, are you in there?" Bob asked, moving his coffee cup back and forth in front of her eyes. "What do you want to do about the police?"

"Oh, Bob, I'm sorry. Please, can't it wait till next week?"

"We have some insurance matters to deal with as well."

"No, Bob. Not now. No way. I just can't deal with any of that now," she said. Her throat tightened up and her eyes brimmed. "You've just got to give me some time." She could no longer hold back the tears.

"Pat, I understand. I lost my best friend, though I can't imagine what it's like to lose a spouse."

"He was my best friend, too."

"I know. I'll put off the police until next week. And I guess we can't really do anything about the insurance until the death certificate is processed, so that can wait too. But Pat?"

"Uh huh?"

"If there's anything Katie or I can do . . ."

"I know. I'll call you. You two have done so much already."

"Nothing more than you and Sam would have done for either of us."

Bob was right, but Pat wasn't sure how she would have made it through the last few days without them.

Pat and Katie covered the 10 miles to the hospital in an eerie silence. But Pat's emotions rode a roller-coaster and her mind filled with questions. How is he? How did this happen? What did that woman on the phone say? Will he be conscious? I should call the children. . . but I don't know anything.

As Katie drove up to the emergency entrance, she told Pat, "I'll go park the car and be right with you." But Pat never heard. She was out of the vehicle and into the hospital leaving the car door as well as Katie's mouth wide open.

"I'm Pat McGrew," she said to the first person she encountered at the desk. "I was told my husband's here. Where is he? I want to see him."

"Mrs. McGrew. Yes. If you'd have a seat, please, I'll let the doctor know you've arrived."

Too nervous to sit, Pat paced in front of the desk. "Is there a phone I might use?"

The woman pointed to a table in the waiting area. "Just dial nine first."

Pat walked to the phone and picked up the receiver. "Who should I call?" she wondered out loud. "Mac? Anne?" Finally, undecided, she simply set the phone back on its cradle, dropped her head into her lap and prayed.

Bob and Katie walked in together, just in time to hear Dr. Whorley introduce himself to Pat. "These are our friends. They're here with me," she said possessively, taking Bob's arm in case the doctor had ideas of excluding them. Dr. Whorley led the group to a private conference room.

"Mom, let's go out for dinner tonight," Mac proposed on Saturday afternoon, bringing his mother back to now. Pat, Anne and Lisa were writing thank you notes at the kitchen table. Pat had drifted silently away.

"Great idea," Anne said. "I think it would do you good to get out of the house."

"Besides, I'm getting tired of casseroles, Jell-O

and chocolate cake," Gregg said.

"I'll call one of the Johnson girls to come stay with Allison," Anne said. "Then we can go somewhere and have a drink and talk about what you're going to do after we all leave tomorrow."

"Oh, I don't know," Pat started to protest.

"You don't have a vote," Mac said. "Anne, call Murphy's and get us a reservation. Let's see, there are si . . .five of us. Make it for 6:30. We can all be ready by then, right?"

"I guess," his mother replied.

Mac was right. It was good to get out of the house. And having a glass of wine with her children helped Pat relax. *I'm so lucky to have them*, she thought. *I only wish they lived closer.*

"So, mom, when are you coming for a visit?" Anne asked later as she passed a bread basket to her mother. "Thanksgiving's only a month away. How about flying out to New Hampshire and spending the Pilgrim's Holiday with us in New England?"

"That's fine, Annie, but then we get her for Christmas," Mac challenged.

"Yes, Pat, we'd love for you to come to California for Christmas. You could help us address the wedding invitations," Lisa laughed. "We have to send them out right after New Years. And of course, we'll all be back here for the wedding in February."

"Will you quit planning my life?" Pat pleaded. "I want to spend some time with all of you, but I'm just not ready to look that far ahead yet. I have tomorrow to get through, and the next day and next week. Right now I want to take it a day at a time. But stay in touch, your propositions interest me," she laughed.

They were finishing dessert when a voice from across the room whined, "Patti, you poor dear, I just heard about Sam today. For God's sake, what happened?"

Pat followed the familiar voice. Her cousin Nettie, dressed in an exotic caftan and obviously slightly intoxicated, was making her way toward their table, her arms spread for an anticipated embrace.

"I'm just back from the Caribbean and Meg tells me Sammy passed away. But she didn't know the details."

Anne and Mac looked at each other and rolled their eyes as they watched their shirt-tail relative hug their mother. She pulled a chair from a nearby empty table, planted herself next to Pat and seized her hand. She glanced around the table and gushed, "my sympathies to you all. Now tell me what happened."

"Oh, Nettie, it was terrible," Pat said with a sigh. "I don't know if I can talk about it yet without crying."

"Well, dear, you just go ahead and cry. It's good to get that out. It's part of the grieving process, you know."

Anne tried to intervene. "Jeannette, maybe mom will feel more like talking next week. We're all leaving tomorrow and I'm sure she'd like some company after we're gone."

"It's okay, Annie," Pat said to her daughter. Then to her cousin, "Sam was out for his usual noontime run, and he was hit by a car."

"They always say that jogging is dangerous," Nettie admonished. "Was he killed instantly?"

Anne elbowed her brother.

Mac stood up. "Nettie, let's leave mother here with the girls. Come on," he said, taking her arm. "Gregg and I'll buy you a drink and fill you in." With the offer of a drink on the table, Jeannette bade Pat farewell with another hug and a promise to stop by next week.

"Just remember, I'm here for you, Patti," she fairly shouted over her shoulder.

"Who is she?" Lisa whispered, watching as Mac and Gregg led the woman away.

Anne started to explain, but Pat never heard.
No, not instantly.
The doctor sat down at the end of the conference

table and Pat sat across from Katie and Bob. He began a clinical review of Sam's situation.

"Your husband was brought to County about, ah, 90 minutes ago, Mrs. McGrew," he said, glancing at his watch. "A witness told the police he was jogging along the river path when a car veered off the road and hit him from behind. The driver was apparently distracted. One of those big paddle-wheel boats was coming up the river on a fall leaf excursion or something, not an everyday event. In any case, your husband never saw the car, never had a chance to jump out of the way. He suffered severe head injuries and was taken immediately to the trauma unit. The paramedics performed CPR all the way from the accident site, but when he arrived here he had no pulse."

"You mean he's dead?" Pat asked, catching her face in her hands and a breath in her throat.

"Well," he continued, "the trauma team worked on him for some time and was finally able to get his heart beating on its own again. They opened an airway in his trachea and intubated him. That's the way things stand now. We're breathing for him."

"Can he recover?"

"It's very severe, Mrs. McGrew, his skull's been crushed and he has a number of other injuries. We haven't completely determined their extent yet."

Pat felt herself go numb. For a moment she felt confused. No thoughts would come together. Then anger welled in her chest. "Then for God's sake, why did you revive him?" *she asked, her voice trembling, yet almost inaudible.*

"It's our procedure," *he said.* "We work to restore the vitals first. Once they're functioning we move on to other organs."

"You don't consider the brain a vital organ?" *Pat asked in astonishment.*

"Of course we do, but without heart and lungs it can't perform at all."

"Can I see him?"

"I think you should . . . "

"I think we should go find the guys and get out of here. We have an early flight tomorrow," Anne said, finishing the last of her coffee. "And I want to make sure Allison is asleep. Otherwise she'll be a crank on the plane."

◆

Chaos ruled the McGrew house Sunday morning. Besides the confusion of packing for four people and a small child, the emotion of the past week was taking its toll. For Pat's sake, Mac and Anne had somehow managed to hide much of their own anguish. Now their grief and guilt at leaving their mother alone came head-to-head with her anticipated loneliness.

"We'll just have to check that stroller and pack those pictures," Gregg said, dragging a suitcase down the stairs.

"But Ali can't walk all the way down the concourse, and I don't want to take a chance of the glass breaking," his wife responded.

"The airline will never let us bring all this carry-on luggage, they have limits, and we need the car seat for her on the plane and her bag of treats and toys. You'll just have to make a choice or they'll make it for you."

"I can ship the pictures, or bring them when I come," Pat offered.

"No," Anne shouted. "I want them with me. They're all I have left of my dad," she cried, planting herself on the bottom step and breaking into tears like she did when she was a child and didn't get her way.

Mac, racing down behind her, shouted, "out of the way, sister, we're going to be late."

Just then Ali came around the corner dragging her doll and shrieking, "Hanna lost her shoe."

All of this was more than Pat's raw nerves could handle. Bursting into tears herself, she joined her daughter on the step and wrapped her in her arms. They sat that way for a long time, sobbing on each other's shoulder until Ali, along with her doll, squeezed in between them and said, "big girls aren't s'pos'ta cry."

Somehow, half an hour later, the entire group and their luggage had made it into the van and was headed to the airport.

Anne and Gregg's plane left first. "Mom, please think about Thanksgiving," Anne reminded as the flight to Boston was called.

"I will." Pat promised, hugging her daughter and son-in-law. "I'll miss you, sweetie. Now you be a good girl, okay?" she said to Allison, picking the child up and burying her face in her hair to hide her tears.

"You be a good Nana too, and don't cry anymore," she said, tapping a tiny finger on her grandmother's cheek. "'Cause I'll see you again real soon."

"Okay, baby. Bye-bye." Pat stood on tip-toe to wave to Allison in her father's arms above the crowd in the jet-way.

An hour later, the scene was repeated on another concourse as Mac and Lisa's flight to Los Angeles was announced. "I'll call you tonight," Mac promised. "And if you need anything at all, please, please let me know."

"I'll do that. And don't worry, Bob and Katie are here for me."

"Yes, I know that, but I really hate leaving you alone."

"You know you're welcome to come for a visit any time, Pat," Lisa offered. "And we definitely want you with us for Christmas."

They chatted about nothing as the line moved toward the gate agent. After hugging Lisa, Pat clung to Mac. "I've gotta go," he said, finally, pulling away. "I love you. I'll call."

As she walked alone through the airport, new tears stung Pat's eyes. "I hate saying good-bye," she muttered. But it's better than not being able to, she thought.

A MESSAGE FROM SAM

Dr. Whorley pulled back the curtain surrounding Sam's emergency room station. Beep. . . beep . . . beep . . . shhh-unk. . . beep. . . beep . . . beep . . . shhh-unk. The heart monitor's signal was punctuated by the respirator forcing oxygen into Sam's chest. Gauze wrappings which swathed his head nearly matched his pasty skin. An ugly bruise swelled his left cheek and his lower lip protruded blackishly. Pat felt her knees weaken and she grabbed for the gurney rail to support herself.

"Dear Lord, is this really Sam?"

"Mrs. McGrew, the friend who usually ran with him didn't today. But he drove by just as the paramedics arrived. He identified him and we also have his wallet . . ."

"Oh, I know, it's Sam," she said, shaking her head and placing her left hand on his, their matching wedding bands next to each other. "It's just . . . he was . . . is . . . such a strong man, so fit, and alive . . . and now he's so . . . oh, all hooked up to these machines." She could barely speak over the emotion gathering in her throat.

"Mrs. McGrew, I think you should spend a few moments here with your husband and then we must talk."

Pat gripped Sam's hand. It didn't move, didn't conform to hers. It felt cold and rigid and lifeless. "You've always been my strength," she said, "now I wish I could pass strength to you." She turned to the doctor. "It's just the *machines functioning . . . he isn't really alive,"* she said, *more as a statement of fact than a question.*

Dr. Whorley nodded. "Our monitors show no brain activity," he added.

"Sam wouldn't want that. I don't want that for him."

"Have the two of you ever discussed it?"

"Yes," she fairly shouted. *"Yes,"* she whispered, *realizing where she was.*

"Mrs. McGrew?"

"Oh, Sam. If only you could come back to me for a little while . . . another hour . . . I could tell you all . . . oh, there's so much I need to tell you . . . "

"Mrs. McGrew?"

" . . . if we could just . . . we didn't get to say goodbye . . . Sam, you've got to know . . . I love you . . . until . . ." She bent and kissed his hand, then let it go. She slowly raised her brimming eyes, then shaking her head, turned abruptly, walked past the doctor and slipped through the curtain. " . . . forever," she finished.

Pat turned the van into her driveway and drove into the garage. "I'll have to sell this thing," she said. "I don't need it and I don't like driving it," stepping sharply on the brake for emphasis.

Rude silence greeted her as she opened the door into her back hall. She shivered facing the emptiness.

"Even this morning's squabbles would be better than this," she said, her voice echoing off the hardness of the appliances in her utility room. "How will I ever adjust to this quiet?" Pat continued into the house, dropping her keys into her purse and catching its strap over the back of a kitchen chair. She hung her jacket in the closet and walked slowly through the house studying the rooms as she went. "There it is," she said, stooping to pick up a doll shoe from under a living-room chair. She wandered downstairs to the family room and dropped herself into Sam's recliner. Opening the drawer in the chair-side table she stared at half a roll of his favorite imported sour lemon drops, then slammed it shut, nearly tipping the table.

Her eyes explored the wall of framed photos over the sofa. They told the McGrew family history. Pat and Sam's wedding, the children's baby pictures, all of them enjoying summer at the lake, school pictures, graduations, Anne and Gregg's wedding, Allison's Baptism, and Mac and Lisa's engagement. "The only thing missing is your funeral, Sam," she said, cynicism seeping through her teeth. "How could you leave me like this?" she whispered.

She sat for a long time, rocking, remembering, her mind playing a video tape of their life together. She recalled the romance of their early years; the fun they'd had with little money, weekends spent rummaging through antique shops for entertainment. The treasures they'd found for next-to-nothing to furnish that first apartment. The joy they had shared when the children came. Sam was delighted with their beautiful daughter, Anne, their firstborn. Pat had wanted a son for him, but he was ecstatic over being a father, no matter what. Then four years later, she got her wish. Steven McGrew II was born, little Mac. Their family was complete. "Oh, Sam . . . you were such a good dad . . . so patient . . . so much more patient than I. Remember the sand castles you built with the kids at the lake? And how you tried to teach Annie's brownie troop to whistle bird calls?

"And what a wonderful husband you were. You never let the spark go out of our marriage." She recalled the poems he'd written for her, the wild flowers he'd picked for her and the music they'd enjoyed together. And later, with more money, how they'd rummaged through shops in Europe on their 25th anniversary trip and had brought back furnishings to decorate their home on the lake.

Whatever will I do now, she wondered. Sam had been her reason for being, her purpose, her whole world. His leaving had collapsed that world and the black hole that remained had drawn the rest of her life into it.

When the ringing phone invaded her reverie, Pat realized the afternoon was gone. She considered letting the machine pick up, but Mac had said he'd call. Could he be home already? She couldn't read her watch in the dim light of the dusk.

"Hello," she said, answering on the fourth ring.

"Pat?"

"Yes."

"It's Father Cooper. We missed you at Mass today. How are you doing?"

"How are you doing?" Father Cooper asked, as Pat walked back into the conference room. "How is Sam doing?"

Pat scanned from Bob to Katie. "How did . . . ?"

"He was visiting a parishioner who's a patient," Bob explained. "I went to get Katie some coffee and ran right into him in the hall."

"Oh, Father, did they tell you how bad it is?"

"They told me about Sam's accident, about his injuries."

"I just saw him. He's. . . he's not . . ." A sob burst from Pat's throat. Bob enveloped her in his arms and pressed her face against his shoulder. She stood that way for a moment, feeling the warmth of her friend. Then, sniffing

back some of her grief, she pulled away and directed her voice at the priest saying, "we've got to set him free. His soul is trapped between heaven and earth. It's being held captive by those damnable machines in there."

Father Cooper and Bob Anders exchanged looks. Katie offered Pat a cup of coffee and then asked tentatively, "what can we do . . . what's going to happen next?"

"I don't know. I don't know if Dr. Whorley is coming here to talk to us about it or what. He was right behind me, I thought."

"Father, what about last rites?" Bob asked.

"Let's see what the doctor says," he deferred. "In the meantime, we can pray." He took an ancient black prayerbook from his pocket, its edges furry from wear. He rustled the tissue pages until he found what he was looking for. "Dear Lord, you said you were going ahead to prepare a place . . ."

"I'm okay," she said, somewhat unconvincingly. "The kids left this morning and things were in total disarray here. I didn't want to miss church, but . . ."

"Would you like some company? I can ask one of the ladies from St. Margaret's Guild to come over."

"Oh, no, Father. I'm fine. I'm really busy," she lied. "Thank you notes and all . . . besides, Katie Anders is just across the back yard if I need anything."

"Well, please take care of yourself. And I expect you at Mass next Sunday," he scolded.

"Oh, don't worry, I'll be there," she promised.

"Well, God bless you, dear. We're all praying for you."

"Thank you for calling, Father. And thanks for being here for us this week. Good night."

Pat hung up the phone and made her way upstairs in the dark. She flipped on the kitchen light and discovered how late it was. "I suppose I should eat something," she said absently opening the refrigerator door. There were several unfamiliar containers left. She lifted the covers and found a noodle casserole she could heat in the microwave. She popped it in and punched the buttons. She started a pot of coffee then went to the cupboard for dishes. She grabbed two plates and some silverware and napkins and carried them to the dining area. She set her place and then walked around the table to Sam's. When she realized what she'd done, purely from force of habit, she slammed the plate angrily onto the table and burst into tears. The phone and the microwave buzzed at the same time, adding to her frustration. She walked back around the corner, grabbed the phone from the wall and sniffled, "hello."

"Mom, what's wrong?" Mac's voice questioned. "You okay?"

"Yes, I'm okay. I just set a place at the dinner table for your father. It just hit me wrong. I guess there are a few things I'll have to get used to." Then, trying to sound more cheerful she asked, "you two make it home all right?"

"Yeah, we had a good flight. I wish we wouldn't have had to leave you alone so soon."

"Well, I may as well get used to it. I'm going to be alone the rest of my life." Pat felt bad the minute she said it. She didn't want Mac to think she was feeling sorry for herself or feel guilty that she was alone. "I didn't really mean that the way it sounded."

"So, what did you do all afternoon?" he asked.

"Oh . . . I talked on the phone, went through the fridge, puttered around here a bit, you know . . ."

"And tonight, what are you going to do tonight?" he continued.

Tonight . . . Pat hadn't really thought about tonight . . . her first night alone in the house. How would she get through it?

"Well, I have some notes to finish up, and the Sunday paper to read, and, well . . . I might call Katie and have her come over for coffee. I just made a fresh pot, and there's all that cake . . . and if I get desperate, there's always Jeannette," she said with a hollow laugh.

"Mom, you're babbling."

"Mac, you know, my dinner just finished in the microwave. I better eat it while it's hot. You can't keep reheating those casseroles."

"Mom, are you really okay?"

"I miss your father, but other than that, I'm fine."

"I miss him too. It's hard to believe I'll never talk to him again."

"Well, I've been talking to him all afternoon. He just doesn't answer, that's all. Mac, I've really gotta go. Now, you give my love to Lisa. Hope you two didn't get too far behind at work being here all week."

"Work is not a problem, mother. It's you I'm worried about."

"Well don't, dear. Okay? Now you take care, and I'll talk to you later in the week."

"Okay, mom. Have a good evening."

"You too, Mac, I love you."

Pat picked at her dinner, sorting hardened noodles from chicken bits and only occasionally taking a bite. She really had no appetite and getting food past the lump in her throat was difficult. Her mind kept replaying Monday afternoon at the hospital.

A MESSAGE FROM SAM

After Father Cooper closed his prayerbook, Pat found herself at loose ends. She walked circles around the conference table. Katie tried to get her to sit, but she couldn't. Finally, Dr. Whorley stepped back into the room. "Mrs. McGrew, I'd like you to meet Janice Reynolds. Janice is our Lifeline Coordinator." *An attractive woman of about 35 in a navy blue dress stepped from behind the doctor and extended her hand.*

"I'm so sorry about your husband, Mrs. McGrew. It's such a tragedy. I know this is a difficult time for you, but I'd like to talk with you about the gift of life."

Pat looked at the woman, crinkling her brow.

"I'm talking about organ donation, Mrs. McGrew."

Pat's hand flew to her mouth and her heart seemed to follow. She didn't know what to say. Her eyes darted from Katie to Bob to Dr. Whorley to the woman in navy blue. She was stunned and overwhelmed by the words.

Katie put her arm around Pat's shoulder. "Come, sit down."

Now Pat was eager to oblige. She wasn't sure her legs would hold her anymore.

Janice Reynolds took a place at the table as well. "Mrs. McGrew," *she began again, folding her hands and looking straight into Pat's eyes,* "as I said, I know this is a difficult time for you, but your husband has given this matter *some consideration. He has an indication on his driver's license marking him as an organ donor."*

"But . . ." Pat had all she could do to keep her voice under control. "But, with all his injuries, are there any organs that can be used?"

"Well, the doctors have done a preliminary assessment, and his most serious injuries are to his head; his heart, kidneys and liver don't appear to be damaged. Organ donation is truly a gift of life, Mrs. McGrew. There are hundreds, actually thousands of people waiting and so many never make it to transplant. But, of course, just because your husband expressed a desire to be a donor does not make it happen. We still need your consent."

"Well, that's obviously what he wanted, but . . ."

Dr. Whorley sat down and, answered the question Pat was afraid to ask. "Mrs. McGrew, there is nothing further we can do for your husband. As you said earlier, it's only the machines functioning in there. And we also need your consent to disconnect them." He opened a file folder and took out a form.

"What about last rites?" she asked, "when can we . . .?"

"Father can administer last rites now and then we can proceed . . ."

Ah, yes, proceed. How could she proceed? In

just those few hours her life had changed. Nothing was the same anymore. She wanted to talk to Sam. She wanted to tell him how she felt, but he wasn't here. She told him anyway. "Yes, I guess I'll have to *proceed* alone, since you're not here to *proceed* with me. But Sam, you promised," she cried, pounding the bed with her fist that night as she tried to sleep.

In fact, they had promised each other — months before when they'd rented the movie. In Ghost, when *that* Sam died, he'd found a way to come back, to let his partner know he was okay.

It had been Sam's idea. *"Let's make a deal," he said, as he cradled Pat in his arms. "If we don't go together — like in a plane crash or a car accident — if one of us dies first, that one has to come back and let the other know they're all right — okay?" he asked, squeezing her shoulder.*

"Don't talk like that," she said. "That's not going to happen. We're going to be together forever, or at least for a very long time."

"I know, at least I hope so. But if something ever did happen to you, I'd want to know that you're okay, where ever you are," Sam said.

"Well, I'd want to know about you too," Pat agreed, humoring him. "But nothing scary," she laughed.

"You mean you don't want me rattling chains under

the bed or jumping out of the closet, or handing you a towel when you step out of the shower? I'd probably do more than hand you a towel," he murmured, stroking her neck sensually.

"It's got to be some kind of message, you know. A surprise, something mysterious," she said, as she turned her face toward his in the dark, now captivated by the concept. "But something real. Something we'd recognize. So there'd be no doubt."

"Yeah, I know what you mean. Of course, who knows what's possible from there, wherever there is, I mean, from some other place."

"Heaven, I'd like to think," she said, then continued, "we'll figure it out. And hopefully we won't need Whoopi Goldberg to help us," Pat laughed. "That woman is too strange. Anyway, you got a deal."

"Some deal!" she shouted into the night. "Sam, where are you?" She buried her face in his pillow and cried herself to sleep.

◆

Pat survived the next few weeks by keeping busy. She tried reading some "coping" books a friend had shared with her, but could not seem to get past the first few pages. Katie was a comfort and Bob had handled the police and the insurance company. There would be a lawsuit, he'd promised, but that was months away. Her finances were in order; her husband had provided well. But she did not seem to be able to get on with her life. She was at loose ends and needed purpose. "Sam," she begged one morning, "tell me what to do."

She cleaned out his closets and dresser drawers. Going through his things was difficult. Even though they'd been married forever, she somehow felt like she was invading his privacy. And she repeatedly found herself brushing away tears or swallowing a lump as pieces of his clothing brought memories flooding back. She recalled the carriage ride in Central Park and Sam wearing the blue patterned sweater he'd bought that romantic weekend in New York. And their Superbowl party when he'd worn a Chicago Bears sweatshirt; he hated the Bears, "but they're from the Central Division," he'd explained. She piled up five or six pairs of running shoes. She'd bugged him for years to throw some of them away — at least the oldest ones. Now, thinking of his last run, she couldn't part with any of them.

She was amused by some of the things he'd saved: Father's Day gifts the kids had made, his college letter jacket. If he'd kept it all these years, how could she possibly give it away? His wedding shoes, worn only once, still in the box. She couldn't bring herself to ask Mac if he'd like to wear them for his wedding, that was just too much symbolism. And finally, after sorting through everything, she couldn't get rid of anything. She wasn't ready. It would be like kicking Sam out of the house. So she just packed it all up and put the boxes in the storeroom. She'd made a huge mess, but she just shut the door on it. Anyway, Sam wasn't around to complain.

As the holidays approached, Pat made plans to be with her kids — Thanksgiving in New Hampshire and Christmas in California, just as they wanted. She decided they were right — it was best to be away from the house and all its memories this time of year. She wasn't sure exactly how she'd get through the season with her traditions shattered. She was definitely not going to decorate or even put up a tree. She simply couldn't. And she almost gave up writing Christmas cards when she had to throw a bunch away after signing them "Sam and Pat McGrew."

Each night . . . she had somehow decided it would come at night . . . she would go to bed alone and wait for Sam's message, some sign, that he was still with her, that he was okay. She would listen for his gentle, whispered "good night, I love you until forever." She would wait to feel his comforting arms wrapped around her when she woke. "I can't believe you're never coming back," she said one morning. "You promised. Remember?" But night after night, morning after morning it was the same. She went to sleep and woke back up alone. Not even in her dreams did Sam return.

Just before Thanksgiving, Pat was out finishing her shopping for Allison. She wanted to take the Christmas gifts to New England when she flew there next Tuesday. She'd recalled the fun she and Sam had last year when they'd bought presents for the little toddler . . . things they knew her parents couldn't afford. She laughed, remembering the hot pink snowsuit they'd chosen. Ali was just learning to talk and Sam had taught her the colors. And when Papa would ask, "what color is your snowsuit, Ali?" She would answer, "foooo-sha." It was just one of his delights.

This year, without someone to share the joy of the season, shopping was a sadder task. But picking out some special things for her little sweetie and imagining the child's face when she opened the packages brightened Pat's mood. In fact, she had actually caught herself humming a carol on the drive home.

She parked the car in the garage, gathered her arms full of the bags of gifts and wrappings from the trunk and pushed her way into the house. The closer pulled the door sharply out of her grasp and slammed it shut behind her. "Sam, I wish you'd fix that so it wouldn't bang so loudly," she said. Then, dropping her purse and purchases on the kitchen table, added, "right." As she passed through the living room to put her coat away, she stopped. She took a deep breath. Then she sniffed the air. There was an aroma of evergreen in the room. It smelled just like it used to when they put the Christmas tree in the front window. But they hadn't put it there for over 20 years; not since they'd finished the family room. "Strange," she muttered.

She hung up her coat, put on a kettle for tea and went to the phone. Katie answered after two rings. "Got time to run over and see what I bought for Ali?"

"I've got writer's cramp from Christmas notes. I can use a break," Kate said kicking out of her boots on the deck.

The two friends fussed over four adorable outfits. "I couldn't decide," Pat explained. "That child is such a doll all dressed up in pretty clothes, but her mother's going to have a fit. Especially when she sees the little bike I ordered. It's being delivered. But Anne won't be able to complain," she laughed. "It's from Santa."

"Clothes are so expensive, I'm sure Anne and Gregg will be grateful," Kate justified as Pat repacked the little outfits in their tissue-lined boxes.

"I've got a question for you. What do you smell?" Pat asked.

"Herbal tea, I guess. What am I supposed to smell?"

"That's it? Nothing Christmassy? Like evergreen or a pine candle?"

"Nooo," she said, sniffing, "nothing like that, why?"

"When I got home, I thought I smelled a Christmas tree in the living room."

"Maybe it was some scent you picked up on your clothes at the mall. They have that Christmas potpourri everywhere these days."

"No, I don't think so. I didn't smell it in the car."

"Well, I don't smell anything but tea. Maybe with all this shopping you've got Christmas on the brain."

"Yeah, maybe."

But that evening when she was turning off the lights before going to bed, she again caught the scent of pine as she passed through the living room. "If I'd been drinking gin I'd have an excuse," she laughed, as she stopped in the bathroom to brush her teeth.

That night, for the first time since his death, Pat dreamed of Sam:

On Christmas Eve the two of them drove up north to their lake cabin to cut down a Christmas tree. When they walked into the woods, they discovered the most perfect tree they had ever seen — a beautiful, completely symmetrical, cone-shaped white pine about 10 feet tall. Each long needle was covered with delicate frost. Together they dragged the tree out of the woods and hoisted it up on top of the car. Back at home, they set it in the living room window. Magically, all the frost remained, even after they trimmed it with hundreds of tiny white lights and golden ornaments. When they finished, the tree positively glistened as thousands of ice prisms reflected each light.

A MESSAGE FROM SAM

When she awoke from the dream, just after dawn, Pat was exuberant. She jumped out of bed like a child on Christmas morning. But as she peeked shyly into the living room, a subtle scent of fresh-cut pine was the only vestige of the dream which had melted like hoarfrost in the light of day. "Silly fool," she scolded, "did you really expect a tree?" But the memory didn't fade, and the joy of seeing Sam, if only as a specter of the night, buoyed her spirits through the holidays. In her mind, that dream was a Christmas gift from Sam.

◆

Between holiday travel and wedding plans, time had evaporated. Now it was February and an unusually early thaw brought with it the promise of spring. So did the baskets of pink tulips that decorated the altar. The McGrew family was all together back at St. Bridget's. Mac and Lisa's momentous day had arrived with glorious sunshine. But as the radiant bride floated down the aisle on billows of ivory lace and her father's arm, Pat's affected smile was as unnatural as the false spring outdoors. She thought she had exhausted her stock of tears during the last four months, but a new supply lay just beneath the surface. And all it took was Mendolssohn's measured cadence to wipe away her control and start the flow. The hurt had begun to heal with time, just like people said it would. Now the gash in her heart ripped open again.

Mac and Lisa reminded Pat of herself and Sam at their wedding: young, full of promise and blissfully in love. She recalled the excitement she felt on that day, nearly 30 years ago, as they started their life together. She thought of Sam. God, how she missed that man. She talked to him every day. He was her last thought before she drifted off to sleep and her first as she woke in the morning. Ever since the Christmas dream, she'd been waiting for another sign, but none had come. She spoke to him silently now: "I wish you were here with me. Aren't you proud of our son? And look at Lisa. Isn't she lovely? What a treasure. She'll make Mac a wonderful wife. I hope neither of them ever has to endure the sadness of losing the other. This isn't fair. Everyone else is here."

The ceremony was concluding. Father Cooper stood a step above the couple he had just united in marriage. "May I present, Mr. and Mrs. Steven McGrew." Then, with a sober look toward Pat, hastily added, "junior. Mac and Lisa." Anne helped Lisa rearrange her train as the congregation applauded. The beaming couple joined hands, smiled at one another and began their walk out of church as the organist entoned the Wagner recessional. When they passed the first pew, Mac slowed to kiss his tearful mother. As he brushed past her ear, he whispered, "I wish dad was with us."

"He is," she responded, "in spirit."

The receiving line formed in the church atrium. Pat stood between Lisa and her father and greeted guests as they filed past. Though the bitter-sweet character of the day tugged her emotions in a hundred directions, mostly she was swept up into the joy of the celebration. Only when a business acquaintance or friend reminded her directly of Sam, did she surrender to tears. Thank God tears are permissible at weddings, she thought. At least I'm not spoiling Mac and Lisa's day.

Later, at the reception, Pat chatted with friends and relatives, danced with her son and her son-in-law and even with Allison, who had pink-and-white balloons from the table decorations tied to each wrist. She looked like a doll dressed in a replica of Lisa's gown. The little flower girl spent much of the evening by her grandmother's side chatting on about how she couldn't wait until summer so she could ride her new bike outdoors instead of in the basement. Pat enveloped her in a big hug and asked, "if I come visit will you show me how you can ride?"

"Oh, please come, Nana, I might not even need my training wheels by then."

For all the planning and work involved with a wedding, the day ended much too soon. Mac and Lisa left in a limo to a rousing chorus of good wishes and headed for the bridal suite in a downtown hotel. They were spending their honeymoon at a ski resort up north before returning to California.

Gregg drove Pat's car home from the Country Club. She sat in back with Ali and supported her head as she dozed in her carseat. "She was so good," Pat said as she looked fondly at the sleeping child and gently stroked her hair.

"She really loves her Nana," Anne responded. "You're so patient with her."

"She's the joy of my life. I just wish you all lived closer so I'd get to see more of her," Pat replied.

When they got home, Pat suggested, "why don't you tuck Ali in and come have a brandy. I'll light a fire."

"She was so tired, I don't even think she woke up when I took off that dress," Anne said as she and Gregg walked down the stairs into the family room. "I thought she'd probably have a fit and want to sleep in it," she continued as she dropped onto the sofa. "How'd you get that fire going so fast?"

"It's a gas log. You just turn the knob."

"When did you get a gas log?"

"Oh, sometime right after Christmas. You know your dad always hauled in wood for our fires and . . ." she sniffed, "I decided this would be easier. I really have used it a lot."

"It makes a nice fire," Gregg said, "you can't tell the difference unless you're close."

"Shall I get the brandy snifters?" Anne asked as her mother took a bottle of Courvosier from the liquor cabinet.

"I've got 'em," Pat replied. "Just dim the lights if you would." She poured the brandy and handed them each a glass. "Cheers," she said, raising hers. Anne and Gregg settled in on the sofa and Pat in the recliner. "This is nice, after all that excitement. What a lovely day."

"It really was," Anne responded. "Those two sure make a great couple. It'll be fun having a sister. I don't think of Lisa as an in-law. Can't wait to see the pictures."

"I only wish Sam could have seen his son married," Pat said quietly.

"I know," Gregg agreed. "Mac said the same thing this morning while we were getting into our tuxes. It was hard being back in that church again."

"Mom," Anne said, swirling her brandy, "I hope this question isn't too painful, but did you ever hear anything about the people who got dad's organs — his heart and liver?"

"And kidneys," Pat said. "No, I just heard that there were four recipients. I think his kidneys went to two different people — out of state somewhere, I think. They didn't tell me their names; privacy issues or something."

"That was really a special thing to do, Pat," Gregg said.

"It was Sam's wish."

"Well, it's a great tribute to dad's memory. Four people are probably alive because of him, and it's kind of nice knowing that part of him is still around," Anne agreed. "I think I'll add that notation next time I renew my driver's license."

"Speaking of tributes, I got an envelope from the

monument people in the mail today. With all the hubbub, I didn't even open it. They were supposed to send me the preliminary design. I'd like to get it done before Memorial Day. I'll be glad to finally have his grave marked. If you're not too tired, let's take a look at what they've sent," she said getting out of her chair and walking over to the desk.

Pat retrieved the large manila envelope and slit it open. She pulled out a folded set of vellum drawings and opened them up. She laid the crackly paper out on the carpet and smoothed out the folds. "Annie, turn up the lights again, please."

Her daughter obliged and joined Pat on the floor. The first sheet was an overall view of the monument and its base, with their dimensions shown. "Before I show you this, I should warn you, that rather than a traditional headstone, I've decided to put in a stone bench."

"A bench?" Anne questioned.

"Yes. I suppose that sounds strange, but I've seen it done before. The monument company suggested that I drive through a cemetery in the city to get ideas on what style, and color and type of lettering I like. I discovered a granite bench under the trees in a very old section. I hiked up the hill and brushed off the snow to take a look. It seemed so peaceful and serene that I decided it was exactly what I wanted. That way, when I visit Sam's grave, I can sit and talk to him . . . maybe even have lunch there in the summer. Anyway, I took pictures and brought them to the contractor," Pat explained. "I suppose you think I'm just a little weird."

"No, mom, it's certainly your choice," Anne said, exchanging raised eyebrows with her husband behind her mother's back.

Pat continued telling them about the color of the stone she had selected. "You know, they start with almost a ton of granite." She described the shape of the bench and how the McGrew name would be carved along the front edge on both sides. She began to demonstrate how their first names, birthdates and the date of Sam's death and eventually her own would be engraved into the seating stone. "Well, here, I'll show you, that must be on this other page," she said, flipping to the second sheet of the drawings. Pat took an involuntary breath.

"What is it, mom? Does it bother you seeing your own name on a gravestone?"

"No, it's not the name at all. It's the words."

"I think it's lovely. It's what dad always said to you . . . what you always said to each other."

"I know. But how did *they* know?"

On a small piece of clear film overlaying the middle of the design, between hers and Sam's names, in a beautiful soft script were the words,

Until Forever.

"This is just bizarre. I didn't ask them to put any words on the stone." She repeated her question, "how did they know?" She retrieved the envelope in which the drawings had arrived and peered into it. A note had remained inside. It read:

"Dear Mrs. McGrew:

Enclosed are the drawings for the bench for your husband's grave. Please review them to make sure everything is correct. If so, please initial each page and return them to us. If you see anything you'd like to change, please note it on the prints.

By the way, our designer took the liberty of adding the words you see on the second page. She saw them on the memorial card you left with us for reference and thought they were most appropriate. If you don't like the idea, they can be eliminated as nothing is yet 'carved in granite.'

We hope to hear from you soon so that

we can complete the project in time for Memorial Day as you wished . . ."

Anne was reading over Pat's shoulder. "You gave them one of dad's memorial cards?"

"Uh huh. It had his name and the dates they needed."

"And it had the words on it too."

"Yes, it did. I guess that's where they got them."

"Well, I like what they've done, mom. The bench idea is growing on me too. I don't know how Mac will feel, but I think you should tell them to go ahead."

"I'll have to think about it, but everything else looks okay. The dates are correct and our names are spelled right. I'll get back to them next week."

"Let's drive out to the cemetery tomorrow, Gregg, and visit dad's grave while we're here," Anne said.

"It is tomorrow," her husband yawned, looking at his watch. "We'd better get to bed, Ali will be awake before you know it. You coming, Pat?" he asked, draining his glass.

"I'll be up in a little bit. I'm going to enjoy the fire for a few more minutes," she said, putting the monument prints back on the desk. "Good night, you two, sleep well."

"Night, mom," Anne said, giving her mother a

hug. "You sleep well, too."

Pat sat back in her chair, sipping brandy and replaying wedding scenes in her mind as she watched the amber flames dance over the fireplace logs. Eventually, Mac and Lisa's wedding merged with her own and in a dream, she and Sam danced until dawn.

They were in a huge ballroom, the only couple on the floor. She was dressed in a beautiful gown and he in elegant formal attire. The orchestra played music just for them. It was wonderful to be in Sam's arms. She felt like Cinderella at the ball, so much in love, sharing an evening with the most handsome man in the world.

She awoke much later to a profusion of kisses being delicately bestowed across her face. "Mmm," she said softly, arching her back and stretching her limbs. "Sam."

"Nana, did you stay up all night?"

"Allison." Pat said tensely as her eyes flew open. Her heart pounded in her chest. Then, taking a deep breath she hugged granddaughter's head against her chest. "What are you doing up so early? Are your mommy and daddy awake," she asked, squinting at the time on the VCR.

"I sneak'ded down to see you, before they wak'ded up," she replied brightly.

"Well, why don't you go get the afghan from the sofa and bring it over here and cuddle with Nana. Aren't you cold?"

◆

A few days later Pat and Katie were sitting at the kitchen table chatting over a cup of coffee and left-over wedding cake when the doorbell rang. Pat returned with an envelope and a big smile. "Guess what I've got? Wedding pictures," she said. "Actually, the proofs. Looks like this envelope can be re-sealed," she said mischievously, "do you think we dare peek?"

"I can't imagine that Mac and Lisa would mind."

"Well I know I can't wait until they get back, and I'm going to want to order some reprints anyway, so I may as well get a head start on picking them out, right?"

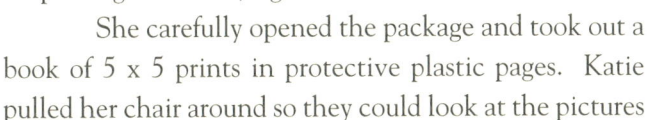

She carefully opened the package and took out a book of 5 x 5 prints in protective plastic pages. Katie pulled her chair around so they could look at the pictures together. "Oohh," she said as Pat opened the book to the first page, a portrait of Lisa in her wedding gown, "isn't she gorgeous? I love her hair that way. Mac looks awfully pleased with himself," she continued as Pat turned the page.

The rest of the photos were in sequence, beginning with candid shots of the bridesmaids getting dressed and the groomsmen and ushers tying each other's bowties. There were pictures of the ceremony and lots of the bride and groom at the reception, drinking punch, cutting the cake and displaying their rings on Lisa's bouquet.

"Look at my little sweetie," Pat said as she flipped a page and encountered a picture of herself dancing with Ali. "She was so much fun. I'm so lonesome for her since they've all gone home."

Toward the back of the book were more formal shots: the bride and groom posed in front of the altar, with Lisa's train arranged in front of them; the entire wedding party also at the altar; Lisa with her mom and dad, Mac with Anne, Lisa and Mac with Ali and the bride and groom with their parents — Janet and Kevin O'Boyle on one side and Pat on the other.

"I think there's something wrong with this one," Pat said, studying the photo.

"What is it?"

"Well look here, next to me," she said, pointing at a spot on the far right side of the print. "There's some funny sort of a glare or something."

"Let me see," Kate said, looking closer. "Where was it taken?"

"In the river room at the country club."

"There are a lot of windows in that room, maybe they reflected some light."

"Possibly, but look here. There are others taken in the same place, there's no glare on them," she said, flipping back to one of Mac and Lisa with Lisa's grandparents.

"Maybe it was the time of day, maybe the sun was at a particular angle."

"No. I distinctly remember when it was taken. It was already dark outside."

"Well, maybe something happened in the processing or maybe it was the end of the roll of film, or maybe his lights malfunctioned, you never know."

"Yeah, maybe, but it looks kind of ghostly to me. I was wishing so hard that Sam could have been with us for that picture, maybe he figured out a way . . ."

"I'd talk to the photographer if I were you," Kate dismissed her friend skeptically. Maybe he has another shot. They usually take more than one in case someone blinks or something. I'll bet he did that and there's a better one."

Later that night when she was alone, before she went to bed, Pat looked through the pictures again, putting sticky notes on the ones she wanted to order for herself. When she came to the one of the bride and groom with their parents, she got out a magnifier. She held the glass at varying heights over the print, but even on closer inspection, could not figure the source of the strange glare on the photo.

"You and I know, though, don't we, Sam," she said. "You were there that day. I told Mac you were. I felt your presence. You'd certainly be at your son's wedding, even if you had to move heaven to do it."

◆

Six months after Sam's death, Pat still wondered if she'd ever recover. Though she didn't cry every day anymore, it could hardly be said she was enjoying life. When friends invited her to join them at concerts or plays or out to dinner, she often felt irrelevant. After all the years as part of a couple, going out with friends as a single person was difficult. The dynamics had changed. The conversations were different.

She tried to settle into the routine of her own schedule. She had gone back to her volunteer work and had even considered getting a real job. But what? She certainly didn't need one with the insurance money and the pending accident settlement. And everything she'd read suggested not making significant lifestyle changes for at least a year after the trauma of losing a spouse. She'd never get over losing Sam, but she longed for the time when she'd adjust. She'd never stop missing him, but she hoped someday she'd come to accept his absence. And she'd never go to sleep at night without expecting a message from him. He'd promised her that.

Now it was truly spring. April had arrived bringing warmer days and budding trees and renewing Pat's energy. She spent many hours in her yard, cleaning up the winter grime. The hard work and fresh air left her exhausted, but it was a good tiredness and she was sleeping better than she had in months.

One evening over the back fence she told Kate, "now that I've got most of the spring work done around here, I think I'll drive up to the cabin next weekend and see what shape it's in. Sam closed it up last fall while I was getting ready for the book sale and of course I didn't go up there at all this winter."

"Why don't you wait a week and Bob and I will come with you? We can help get the dock in and clean up the beach. Bob's sister and her family are coming so we can't go this weekend."

"Oh, I'm not planning to do any of that heavy stuff yet. You guys will get your chance to help with all that sometime in May. I just want to see if there was any damage over the winter. There's a handy-man from town I can hire to do any repairs that are needed. He's worked for us before, but he gets booked up if you don't contact him early in the season. And I thought maybe I'd go through some of Sam's things and I want to do some thinking about the future. It's a good place for reflection."

"Are you sure you want to be up there all alone? It's your wedding anniversary, isn't it? Your first one without Sam. Won't that be hard for you?"

"That's part of why I'm going," she whispered, emotion gathering in her throat. "I have such good memories of Sam and me at the lake. I refuse to hide from them, or to ignore the significance of the date, even though he's not here."

"You're one tough lady, Pat McGrew," Kate said, squeezing her friend's shoulder across the fence.

"What choice do I have?" she asked, wiping away a tear in the half-darkness.

"Well, if you decide you need to talk to someone, give us a call. With Sally and the kids here, we should be home all weekend."

Saturday morning dawned with an overcast sky, but Pat didn't mind. She had packed the night before and after a shower and a quick cup of coffee and toast, she loaded the car with a few provisions and her suitcase. Once she reached the countryside, she popped a bestselling book-on-tape into the car's cassette player and got lost in three hours of political intrigue.

It was nearly noon when she parked in front of the general store in the small town which served the Willow Lake area where the McGrew's cabin was located. It was cool, but the sun had come out, promising a nice weekend. A bell at the top of the door announced her arrival into the combination grocery/hardware/liquor store. Judy Olson, the proprietor, came out from the back room and greeted her warmly. "Well, well, how ya doin' Miz McGrew? Ain't seen you 'round here since last summer. Saw your husband last fall, came in for a hack-saw blade as I recall. Say, where is that good lookin' man?" she asked, squinting to try and see out the front door.

"I guess you haven't heard," Pat said softly. "Sam was killed last October."

"Noooo! Huntin' accident?"

"He was struck by a car, actually."

"I'm sorry, I didn' know. You poor lady. He was a nice man. My sympathies to ya," she said, coming around the counter to give Pat a hug. "I don't know what I'd do without my Ralph, the big lug."

"Thank you, Judy. It happened just a week or so after he closed the cabin for the season."

"So yer up here to open 'er up all by yerself, is that it?"

"Well, that's my plan," Pat responded.

"Well, if you need anythin' out ta the lake, you jus' let us know. Ralph'll be right out ta help ya."

"I'll surely do that. Now, I do need some eggs and milk and a bottle of that wine we always liked."

Twenty minutes later, Pat turned her car into a wooded side road which led to their cabin. After a short drive, she caught sight of the low slung, natural wood cottage with a shake roof poised amid a stand of still-bare birch trees, their white bark shining in the sun. Stopping the car in the driveway, she put it in park, folded her arms over the steering wheel and stared for a moment out at the shimmering water beyond. Willow Lake. Their lake. She and Sam had rented cottages here for a few years before they could afford to build their own. They had come here for at least 25 years. If she closed her eyes, she could almost see Annie running along the beach with her sand pail, and little Mac standing on the dock with his fishing pole. And Sam . . . well, she'd think about Sam later.

She retrieved her overnight bag from the trunk and climbed the three steps to the cabin door. She unlocked it and turned the knob. It took some nudging to open it, but it always stuck a little in the spring. A musty, closed-up smell greeted her and she dropped her bag into a chair and walked over to the patio door. She removed the security bar, opened it and stepped out onto the deck, breathing the fresh, crisp air. "That's better," she said, going back in. She picked up her bag and continued into the bedroom to open its door as well. "It'll probably get it so cold in here, I'll need the heater later," she laughed, "but the lake air sure feels good."

She went back to her car and got the cooler, the bags of food and her wine and carried them into the house. She turned on the electricity, the water and pump, the refrigerator and the hot water heater, then changed into work clothes and began putting things away. Sam had done a great job of tidying up in the fall. Everything was neat and in its place, just a little dusty. She put her suitcase in the closet and took out a lawn-chair. She noticed their windsock hung on a hook. The cabin owners hung them from their houses or decks or out on their docks to let each other know they were *at the lake*. "I think I'll just leave it in the closet until the dock gets in. I'm not advertising my stay here this weekend," she said.

Pat made a sandwich and took it out on the deck. "Might as well enjoy the weather," she said, sitting in the lawnchair with a plate in her lap. She'd haul the patio table out of the storage shed when Kate and Bob came up to help in May. She finished her lunch and reclined the chair a bit to catch a few rays and dozed off for a few minutes.

She awoke with a start when she heard someone calling her name. "Pat, how are you?" It was Jack Emerson from the cottage next door, making his way between the trees across the lawn. "Judy at Olson's in town said you were up here. Oh, did I disturb you?" he asked as he got closer.

"Hello, Jack, she said, sitting up straighter. "No, you didn't disturb me. I just had some lunch and was enjoying the sunshine trying to decide which of my projects to tackle first."

"Pat, Judy told us about Sam. I don't know what to say. I'm so sorry."

"I don't know what to say either. There is nothing left to say."

"Well, how are you doing?"

"Pretty well, I guess. I have good days and bad days. I miss him terribly, but I feel like he's around me somehow, you know, his spirit. That's why I came up here. He always loved it here. We always loved it here."

"I wish you'd have called. We would have come to the funeral."

"It all happened so fast. I couldn't even think of whom to call, besides the kids of course. Can I get you a chair? Something to drink?"

"No, no. I just saw you out and wanted to express my sympathy. Jane doesn't even know I'm gone. I'm supposed to be picking up sticks in the yard. Not my favorite task."

"I've about decided to do one of my least favorite, windows. I never much like doing it, but it makes everything look cleaner. I think I'll start on the outside while it's warm. I can do the insides later."

"Well, I better get back at it before the boss finds me gone."

"Tell her hello for me."

"I will." Then he continued, "and Pat, I'm truly sorry, we both are," he said, bending to give her a hug. "It's just so unbelievable that he's gone." Then, straightening up, he turned his head quickly away and, in an emotion-laden voice said, "maybe we can have a glass of wine later,"

"Yeah, maybe."

"It'll be just like old times . . . well, not exactly," he said over his shoulder, as he started back across the grass.

Pat busied herself with her window project. First the kitchen windows, then the large patio doors across the front of the cabin which led to the deck, then the bedrooms. She hosed off the screens and replaced the storm windows. When she'd finished outside, she moved inside. She put a CD into the player she'd brought and made her way around the house dragging her scrub pail and wiping cloths with her. She stepped back to admire her work. "It looks so much brighter, almost like the outside has come inside," she said, looking toward the lake and noticing how little daylight was left. "And it's getting cold," she said as the music ended. "Think I'll dump the bucket, get cleaned up and fix some supper." She emptied the scrub water and closed up all the windows.

She was standing at the sink peeling carrots for a salad when she heard the sound. The blinds she had opened earlier when she cleaned the window by the table rattled slightly, but in the silent cabin any noise was loud. Startled for a moment, she turned to look. "Hmph, I must have dislodged some dust mites." She turned back to the sink and peeled another carrot. The blinds clicked again. This time, she wiped her hands, walked to the window and looked out. The sun had just set leaving the sky above the lake vividly painted with every shade from deep purple to crimson to orange to bright yellow. And all of the colors repeated as a reverse spectrum in the water, moving toward duskiness at the shore. Pat's face reflected the radiance. "Sam," she sighed deeply, "you would not let me miss something as spectacular as this, would you." She stood by the window for a long time, until the colors had almost faded into darkness, and thought about Sam and about how 30 years ago tomorrow she had become his wife.

  A knock on the door finally disturbed her thoughts. "Pat," Jane Emerson shouted through the open screen door, "You there?"

  "Yeah."

  "We're just about to put some steaks on the grill. Want to join us, or have you already eaten?"

  "I was just putting a salad together."

  "Well bring it along. I forgot to buy lettuce."

  "Okay. Sounds pretty good. I'll bring my bottle of wine, too. I think I'd like a glass right about now."

  Pat enjoyed the evening with her lake friends. She and Sam had known the Emersons for a number of years and they reminisced over their many fun times together. Jane and Jack were deeply saddened by Sam's death, and when Pat shared some of the details of the accident, they expressed their philosophy of enjoying even the simplest pleasures in life because, as Jack put it, "you just never know how many big ones you'll get."

"Speaking of which, did you see the sunset?" Jane asked.

"Wasn't it magnificent?" Pat responded. "Sam and I used to sit on the deck and watch them. That was one of our favorite lake things. We had some really special times here."

Over homemade apple pie and coffee, Jane asked, "so what are your plans for the future?"

"That's something I've been trying to come to some resolution about. I feel so . . . so unfocused, so undirected. Like I did when I started college . . . just before I met Sam, as a matter of fact. I keep waiting for an inspiration, but the problem with inspiration is its unpredictable timing, I don't know how long I might have to wait," she laughed.

After dessert and more conversation Jane and Jack walked Pat back to her cottage. She was tired from all the work she'd done and from the fresh air.

"Thank you both for a lovely evening," she said giving them each a hug. "It was much more fun than salad alone. Maybe I'll see you tomorrow before you head out. I'm staying until Monday. I have some more chores to get done around here."

"Good night, Pat. Sleep well. And don't work too hard."

She did sleep well, and long. It was nearly 10:00 AM before she awoke. And when she did, as usual, her first thoughts were of Sam. She felt particularly close to him today and not at all sad. "Good morning, love," she said. "I guess you know about it being our anniversary. Thirty years, on April 30th, as a matter of fact. Is that supposed to be golden or something, like a birthday? Is that what showing me that golden sunset was all about last night? Sure was beautiful. Wish you'd have been here to enjoy it with me. I miss you, you know. And I'll always love you, until forever."

She got up, made coffee and scrambled eggs and toast, got dressed and started on her projects. Today she intended to vacuum and dust and to look through Sam's lake clothes to see what she'd keep and what she'd give away. She got the cleaning done in the morning and in the afternoon started to dig through dresser drawers and closets. She sorted the give-aways from the throw-aways, but mainly just organized. She decided to save some old work shirts for herself. Maybe she'd take up painting again, and some of them would come in handy.

She'd been sitting on the floor most of the afternoon and when she stood up to put the drawers back in the dresser, realized how stiff her legs had gotten. "Maybe a walk down by the beach will help get the circulation back." As she stepped out onto the deck, she was blasted by a stiff breeze blowing in from the lake. "Better wear something warmer. It's not summer yet."

Pat went back in and looked in the closet. Sam's old red and black plaid wool jacket was hanging in front of her. "This'll work," she said, taking it from the hanger. As she put it on, she was nearly overcome by the sensory power of the garment. Its collar was imbued with Sam's scent and the rough wool chafed her cheeks like his weekend beard. Were his arms around her? Her heart hammered in her chest. She struggled for breath. She was electrified, trembling, suddenly light-headed. She had to sit down.

She fell into a chair, dropped her head into her lap and sobbed. "Sam, you're here, aren't you? Oh, where? Where? Please, please come back."

How long had she sat there? She wasn't sure. She only knew it was nearly dark. She stood up, turned on a light and stumbled into the bathroom to bathe her swollen eyes in cold water. She felt chilled, shaky. She came back to the living room, closed the patio door and sat back down in the chair. "I thought I was past this," she berated herself. She was still cold. She pulled her knees up to her chest. Huddling against herself, she shoved her hands into the pockets of Sam's jacket for warmth.

"What's this?" she asked, pulling out a mass of loose-leaf paper wrapped around a pencil and some crumbling maple leaves. She unfolded the clump and smoothed it out in her lap. It contained several pages of Sam's familiar scrawl. She perused it for a moment, deciding it was one of his poems. She began to read.

Together

We are one you and I, like two sides of a coin,
bonded by the strength of love, a tie by heaven made.
Stay with me my darling, and let me gaze upon you
'til sight is gone, the flame is out
and life completely fades.

Grow with me my love, and let me share your dreams.
Together we will sing through life awash in utter joy.
A partnership of senses,
unspoken words discovered.
Souls wrapped in one another, giving fervent feelings voice.

A MESSAGE FROM SAM

And if one must leave the other, let it happen when we're old,
when we'd never know the emptiness of being here alone.
When the dimming eye of aging keeps absences unnoticed
and deafness leaves a tiptoed exit
silent and unknown.

And if the seeker comes for one, I pray that it be me.
By myself I wouldn't make it through one day.
Seismic force would rip my breaking heart from out my chest
and raging tears would flood
the very chasm in its place.

And when your earthly day is ended too,
I'll wait for you at twilight,
to wrap my soul around yours
somewhere else in time and space.
And delighting in the wonder, serene, once more completed,
I'll watch as rays of amber cast their splendor on your face.

Then joined until forever, we'll glide through glorious meadows,
two feathers on the wind,
two leaves across a frozen lake.
For we're meant to be together,
eternally together.
A spirit seamed in oneness, that heaven won't
forsake.

Another chill moved up her back and froze the hairs on her neck. But she couldn't cry. She was completely out of tears. Somehow she was comforted and finally felt at peace. "Sam, Sam, Sam, what a beautiful anniversary gift. What a beautiful sentiment. When did you write this? That weekend when you were here without me? Just before . . . ? Did you know? Have some sort of premonition?"

She read the poem again, this time out loud, stopping after certain lines to ponder their significance. "Oh, how I too wish we could have grown old together, I always thought we would," she said. "And I wish I had been the first to go. You don't know the struggle I'm going through, Sam. Or maybe you do. I know you are out there somewhere and you'll be waiting for me when it's my turn. Then we will be together until forever. You did keep your promise."

◆

Pat drove back to the city the next afternoon. The weekend had left her exhilarated. She avoided the freeway and took the country roads home, singing as she went. Now she could work on putting some direction in her life. Preoccupied, she drove right past the cemetery without realizing it. I should visit Sam, she thought, seeing where she was. She pulled into the first available driveway and turned around. Passing through the old gate, she noticed the trees. Just over the weekend their buds had burgeoned into the vaporous green froth of springtime. That's the way I feel, she thought, reborn. Her car bounced along the ruts in the grass as she drove toward Sam's resting place. "The bench is in," she shouted, looking up at the gray granite monument that marked his grave. She parked as close as she could, jumped out of the car and bounded the rest of the way up the hill.

She inspected the bench, appraising the craftsmanship and the fine veins of black rippling through the light gray of the granite. She ran her finger over every letter of their name etched on the edges of the stone. She stood back a few feet and admired the graceful curve of the support legs. She studied the seat and nodded her head. "I did the right thing. Right, Sam?" Then, seating herself on the shiny surface, said, "gotta try it out. A little hard, but it sure is smooth." she added, sliding back and forth. She opened her purse and pulled out the poem Sam had left her. She turned sideways, straddled the bench and spread the papers out in front of her. As she was re-reading Sam's words for the fifth or sixth time, she was distracted by a snapping twig. She followed the sound with her eyes.

A young man was walking between two rows of graves just beyond her car, stopping at each, reading the monuments as he went. Pat watched him for a moment. "Looking for someone in particular?" she called out. "I come here a lot, maybe I can direct you."

"McGrew," he said, "Steven A. McGrew?"

"Up here." she said, "Steven McGrew . . . Sam, is . . . was my husband. Do I know you or do you know my kids?" she asked, noticing his age.

"I don't think so," he said, climbing the hill and

stopping next to the bench. He stared at the name on its side. "I couldn't see that from down there," he said, pointing. "Your car blocked my view. I feel kind of like a detective, trying to solve a riddle," he added, slightly out of breath.

"And Sam's in your riddle?"

"Well . . . ah . . . actually, I don't know. I've been trying to piece a puzzle together, you know, through newspaper clippings and accident reports and obituaries, matching dates," he said, pulling a bundle of tattered papers from his pocket. And then I talked to the caretaker at this cemetery."

"So, what's the puzzle?"

"Ah . . . well . . . um . . . I don't know for sure," he said, suddenly nervous. "But . . . ah . . . I think . . . anyway, I'm fairly certain that . . . ah . . . I'm . . . well . . . alive today because of him."

"What do you mean?"

"I kind of feel like an adopted kid looking for a birth parent."

Pat's head turned sharply and she looked up at the person standing above her.

Immediately realizing the implication of what he'd just said, the young man quickly continued. "What I mean is . . . I think I've got his heart. The hospital wouldn't give me a name."

Pat relaxed, shook her head and arched her eyebrows. "And you traced him here?"

"Yes. I wanted to visit his grave to somehow honor what he did. The doctor said I'd be dead within three weeks without the transplant. You're . . . Patricia?" he asked, twisting his head to read her name on the part of the bench that he could see.

"Yes, Pat McGrew," she said, extending her hand.

"Jeff Burney," he said, taking it. "And Steven McGrew was your husband?"

"Sam. He went by Sam, his initials." Then she asked, "so, how's your health now, how do you feel? Everything working?"

"Oh, yes. I feel great, better than I've felt in years — re-born, actually. I was on that list for almost a year, sitting around, waiting. Toward the end it got pretty bad. Then the call finally came, and now I'm alive. And life sure is sweet."

"And you're able to do everything you did before?"

"Well, I'm working . . . for Lifeline, as a matter of fact. Trying to make transplants happen for other people," he said, smiling broadly. "I'm just volunteering right now, but they've promised to hire me as a coordinator soon."

Pat turned her eyes skyward. "Ah, yes," she said emphatically.

Jeff continued, "can I ask you a question?"

"Sure."

"Did you . . . was he the . . . oh . . . do I have his heart?"

She thought for a moment before answering. "I'll always believe that I have his heart," she said. "He gave it to me 30 years ago. But," she said, continuing, "as for your transplant, we donated Sam's organs, if the dates match . . . "

"I checked. They do, Mrs. McGrew, they do." He paused for a moment, then added, "I don't know how to thank you."

"It's what he wanted."

"But you had to make the decision. I'll be grateful to you, until . . . well . . . forever."

Pat smiled up at Jeff, and wiped away a single tear that had drained from her eye. "Until forever, hmm?" she said quietly, gathering her papers and getting up from the bench. "Until forever," she whispered, reading the words where she'd been sitting. Then, turning back to Jeff, she looped her arm through his and they walked together down the hill. "So tell me about working for Lifeline," she said. "Would I need a lot of training?"

Until Forever

About the Author

Nancy Schriefer, a marketing executive in St. Paul, Minnesota, wrote *A Message From Sam* based on inspirations she experienced after the death of her daughter. She is currently working on a collection of poetry and short fiction.

Since sharing this story with family and friends, she has learned of many others who've experienced messages of hope and strength they attribute to departed loved ones.
If you have such a story you're willing to share, please contact the author at the address below to be included in a future anthology.

Escape Key Press
245 E. 6th Street
St. Paul, MN 55101

Acknowledgments:

To all of my friends and family who encouraged me in this
adventure, I am infinitely grateful.
In particular, special thanks to my husband for his continuing
love and support.
To my mother-in-law, Margaret, for exacting a promise to "finish."
To my editor, Carol Ratelle Leach, for her words of wisdom.
To my designer, Patty Gardner, for her creativity.
To Barbara Deese of my writing group for her critique and input as
someone who's "been there."
To my friend and associate, Becky Amble,
for being a sounding board and brainstorming partner.
And of course, to Kristin, for her inspiration from . . .
well . . . from somewhere else.